The Anti-Circus Crew

Written by Nicole Schubert

Illustrated by Galina

A circus train pulled into town.

The elephants, the tigers and also the clowns.

To some it is an unwelcome sound.

A certain group of kids refuse to see the show.

They have learned things about the circus that most kids don't know.

The kids all gathered to make a plan.

They're making posters and signs, whatever they can.

Life in a circus is a real pity.

The days are long traveling from city to city.

The animals are chained by their leg - no room to move about.

Locked in a cage all day - hardly ever getting out.

Elephants often have to give rides.

It hurts their back with every stride.

The trainer makes animals learn silly tricks.

If they don't do them right - they are poked with sharp sticks.

Tigers have to jump through flaming hoops.

While little kids lick their ice cream scoops.

Bears ride around on little bikes too.

It is not a natural thing they do.

Circus animals have to perform whether they want to or not.

Even when they are sick- noses running with snot.

The circus would be great with only acrobats and clowns.

That would make the animals smile - instead of frown.

Life in the circus is no fun at all.

It is not enjoyable - it is not a ball.

They spend most of the year traveling by train.

They dream of their freedom on an endless grassy plain.

"Why do people attend the circus- when it is so sad?"

"Seeing animals live this way makes me very mad!"

Take a stand against the circus - be a true friend.

Let's all work together to see the circus END!

The next time the circus comes to your town,

be prepared and gather all your friends around.

The animals are rooting for all you can do.

Help them out by organizing an Anti-Circus Crew too!

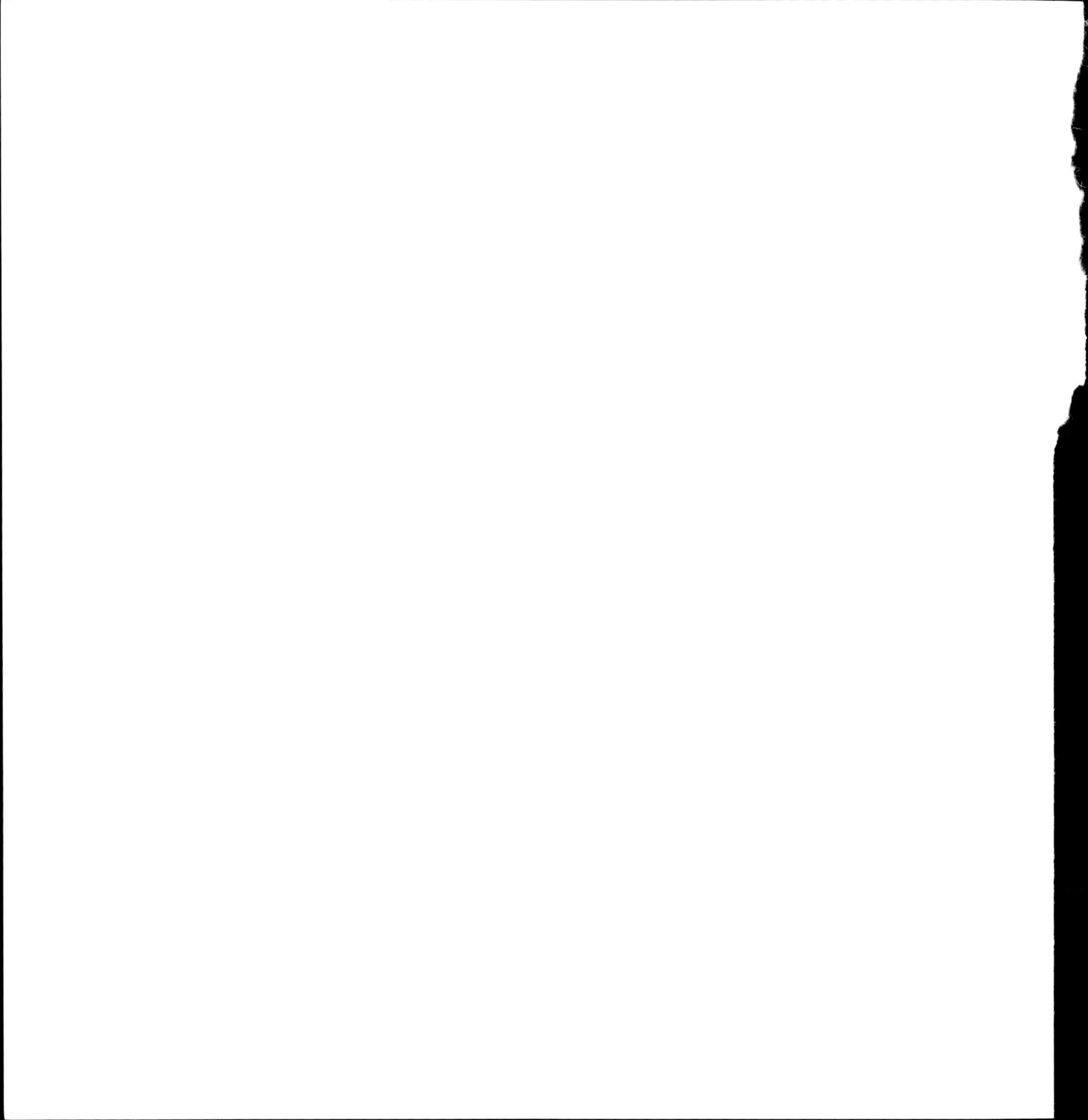